How do You Sleep?

Elspeth Graham

Contents

Oxford

Oxford University Press, Great Clarendon Street, Oxford, OX2 6DP

Oxford New York

Athens Auckland Bangkok Bogota Buenos Aires
Calcutta Cape Town Chennai Dar es Salaam Delhi
Florence Hong Kong Istanbul Karachi Kuala Lumpur
Madrid Melbourne Mexico City Mumbai Nairobi Paris
São Paulo Singapore Taipei Tokyo Toronto Warsaw

and associated companies in
Berlin Ibadan

Oxford is a trade mark of Oxford University Press

Text © Elspeth Graham 1999
Published by Oxford University Press 1999
A CIP record for this book is available from the British Library

ISBN 0 19 915752 9
Available in packs
Pack A Pack of Six   (one of each book)   ISBN 0 19 915756 1
Pack A Class Pack   (six of each book)   ISBN 0 19 915757 X

Acknowledgements

The publisher would like to thank the following for permission to
reproduce photographs: Bruce Coleman Collection/John Cancalosi:
p 6; Bruce Coleman Collection/Jens Rydell: p 4; Corbis UK
Ltd/Michael & Patricia Fogden: p 7; Corbis UK Ltd/Wolfgang
Kaehler: p 1; Corbis UK Ltd/George McCarthy: p 5; Corbis UK Ltd/
Scott T Smith: p 3; Oxford Scientific Films/David Fleetham: p 8;
Oxford Scientific Films/Raymond Mendez: p 9; Planet Earth
Pictures/Jonathan Scott: p 10; John Walmsley: p 11.

Front cover photograph by Corbis UK Ltd/Dan Guravich
Back cover photograph by Corbis UK Ltd/Yann Arthus-Bertrand

Printed in Hong Kong

Animals sleeping

Animals need to rest every day.
Most animals sleep.

3

Bats

Bats sleep upside down.

Bats sleep during the day.

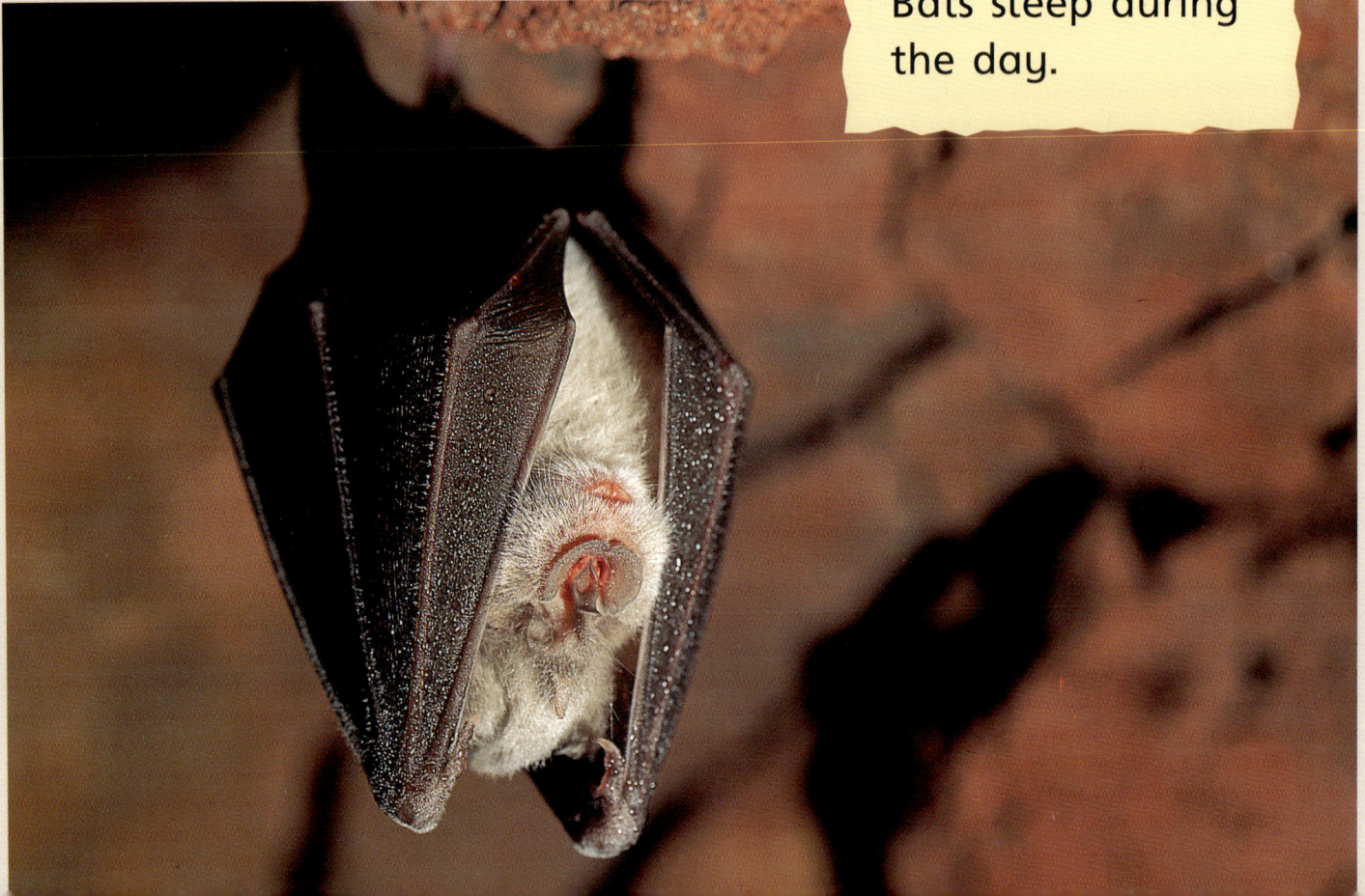

Dormice

Dormice sleep curled up like a ball.

Dormice sleep
all winter.

5

Snakes

Snakes sleep with their eyes open.

This snake looks as if it is awake, but it is asleep.

Flamingoes

Flamingoes sleep on one leg.

They tuck the other leg out of sight.

7

Sharks

Some sharks swim along when they sleep.

If this shark stops
swimming it will die.

Ladybirds

Ladybirds sleep with lots of other ladybirds.

Ladybirds hibernate in the winter.

Hippopotamuses

Hippopotamuses sleep standing up in the water.

They sometimes use each other for pillows.

You

How do you sleep?

Index